# Gardeners

## The Ultimate Collection of Gardening Jokes

Published by Glowworm Press
7 Nuffield Way
Abingdon OX14 1RL
By Chester Croker

## Jokes for Gardeners

These jokes for gardeners will make you giggle. Some of the gags are old, some are new, and while we don't want to plug them too much, we hope you enjoy our collection of the very best gardening jokes and puns around.

These funny gardening jokes will have you laughing all the way to the potting shed.

# DEDICATION

This book is dedicated to the truly wonderful Jean Christensen.

She has green fingers and green thumbs, and her plants grow bigger and healthier than anyone else I know.

Table of Contents

## Chapter 1: Gardener Jokes

In this book you will find corny gardener jokes that will hopefully make you laugh. Some of them are old, but some of them are new, and we hope you enjoy this collection of the very best gardening jokes and puns around.

We've got some great one-liners to start with, plenty of quick-fire questions and answers themed gags, some story led jokes and as a bonus some cheesy pick-up lines for gardeners.

This mixture of gardening jokes is guaranteed to get you laughing.

## Chapter 2: One Liner Gardener Jokes

My wife said she's leaving me because of my unhealthy obsession with plants. I said where's this stemming from petal?

---

I tripped over the garden path yesterday and landed in the herb section. I guess I must have fallen on hard thymes.

---

A weed is a plant that has mastered every survival skill - everything that is except for learning how to grow in rows.

---

On my first day of school my gardening mad parents dropped me off at the wrong nursery. There I was surrounded by trees and bushes.

---

I used to have a job making furniture out of plants. It was no bed of roses though.

Knowledge is knowing that a tomato is a fruit; and wisdom is knowing not to put it in a fruit salad.

---

A gardener friend of mine gave me some great advice, saying I should put something away for a rainy day. I've gone for an umbrella.

---

I got called pretty today and it felt good. Actually, the full sentence was, "You're a pretty bad gardener." but I'm choosing to focus on the positive.

---

I went to a round table talk the other day at my local gardening club. It was ridiculous; I couldn't get a word in hedgeways.

---

I went online and searched for "foolproof easy to grow garden plants."

Nothing came up.

Professional gardeners have a hard time. They earn a meager celery, come home beet, and just want to turn-ip the covers, en-dive into bed.

---

Those who plant trees really be-leaf in the future.

---

Did you hear about the cross-eyed landscape gardener who got sacked because he couldn't see eye to eye with his customers.

---

I saw I had an empty patch in the garden. So, I planted a rose bush there and I said to myself, 'Thistle do.'

---

I'm not aging, I just need re-potting.

I heard on the news that a burglar had used a potato to smash a window, but he said the evidence was planted.

---

Yesterday, a male gardener's wife asked him to pass her lipstick but he passed her a super-glue stick instead by mistake. She still isn't talking to him.

---

So if flowers have both male and female parts, but it's the bees that do the pollinating, surely that makes it some kind of threesome.

---

I was prudently examining my tomato plants today looking for caterpillar tracks. Then I got run over by a tank.

---

Did you hear about the guy who stole a calendar from the gardening store? He got twelve months.

---

I wouldn't kill so many of my houseplants if they could scream for food like my kids do.

My pretty next door neighbor has a beautifully maintained garden. Whenever she needs help with the gardening, she goes out in a short skirt, bends over to pick some weeds and she soon has plenty of willing helpers.

---

I hate my part time job as a leaf blower, the pay is terrible. But if I was a gardener, I would be raking it in.

---

Did you hear about the miracle of the blind gardener? He picked up a hammer and saw.

---

I was cutting the lawn this afternoon when a frog intentionally threw himself under my lawn-mower. I guess he wanted to Kermit suicide.

---

I've planted a bay tree in my garden.

I can't wait until it grows its first window.

The drought prevention officer said they'd had an anonymous tip-off that I'd got a sprinkler. I said yes, you would too if you had prostate cancer.

---

I read in the paper about a man who died following a nasty accident with a lawnmower. They had to do a *com-post* mortem.

---

A neighbor of mine is not the sharpest tool in the box. She hung a raincoat on top of her apple tree after someone told her she should get an Apple Mac.

---

I'm quite annoyed about this hose pipe ban. It will have to start jet washing my lawn from 30 yards away.

---

I was really impressed by the scarecrow I saw the other day.

He was out standing in his field.

## Chapter 3: Question and Answer Gardener Jokes

Q: What do you get if you divide the circumference of a pumpkin by its diameter?

A: Pumpkin pi.

---

Q: What vegetable can tie your stomach in knots?

A: String beans.

---

Q: What kind of socks does a gardener wear?

A: Garden hose.

---

Q: Why would The Incredible Hulk be a good gardener?

A: He has very large green fingers.

---

Q: Why did the absent minded gardener plant some of his cash?

A: Because he wanted his soil to be rich.

Q: What insect is musical?

A: A humbug.

---

Q: What kind of vegetable do you get when an elephant walks through your garden?

A: Squash.

---

Q: What grows when fed but dies when watered?

A: Fire.

---

Q: Why did the tomato blush?

A: Because he saw the salad dressing.

---

Q: Why did the cannibal landscaper get fired?

A: For buttering up his customers.

---

Q: Why are some husbands like lawn mowers?

A: They can be difficult to get started, emit foul smells, and they don't work much of the time.

Q: How do you compare apples and oranges?

A: By their nutritional value.

---

Q: What do you call a gardener who is happy every Monday morning?

A: Retired.

---

Q: What gets larger the more you take away?

A: A hole.

---

Q: Have you heard about the garlic diet?

A: You don't lose much weight at all, but you look thinner from a distance.

---

Q: What do you call a grouchy, bad-tempered gardener?

A: A snap dragon.

---

Q: What do you get if you cross Lassie with a rose?

A: A collie-flower.

A few for the kiddies:-

Q: What sort of flowers would you give to King Tut?

A: Chrysanthemummies.

---

Q: Why did the gardener quit his job?

A: Because his celery wasn't high enough.

---

Q: What do you call a land where people drive around in pink cars?

A: A pink car-nation.

---

Q: What do you call it when worms take over the world?

A: Global worming.

---

Q: What happened when a gardener crossed a chili pepper, a shovel and a terrier?

A: She got a hot-diggity-dog.

Q: Why was the cucumber mad?

A: Because it was in a pickle.

---

Q: What exactly is a Honeymoon salad?

A: Lettuce alone, with no dressing.

---

Q: What do you get if you cross a four-leaf clover with poison ivy?

A: A rash of good luck.

---

Q: What do you call a mushroom that is the life and soul of the party?

A: A fun-guy.

---

Q: What grows under your nose?

A: Tulips.

---

Q: Where is a good place to send kids to grow?

A: Kinder-garden.

Q: Why don't you ever iron a four-leaf clover?

A: You might press your luck.

---

Q: What do you get if you cross a gardener with a pair of headphones?

A: Beets by Dre.

---

Q: What does the Green Giant wear to a business meeting?

A: A three peas suit.

---

Q: Who is funnier than a goofy gardener?

A: A Jolly Rancher.

---

Q: What water yields the most beautiful and bountiful vegetable garden?

A: Perspiration.

## Chapter 4: Short Gardener Jokes

A Brit, a Frenchman and a Russian are studying a painting of Adam and Eve in the Garden of Eden.

"Look at their reserve, their calm," ponders the Brit. "They must be British."

"Non," the Frenchman disagrees. "They are naked, and they are so beautiful. Undoubtedly, they are French."

"Nyet," the Russian states. "They must be Russians - they have no clothes, no shelter, have only an apple to eat; and they are being told they live in paradise."

---

A woman applying for a job in a lemon grove appeared far too qualified for the job.

The foreman asked if she had experience in picking lemons to which she replied "I sure have – I've been married and divorced three times."

---

The homeowner was delighted with the way the gardener had done all the work on his overgrown garden and said "You did a great job, and here's an extra 50 dollars to take the missus out to dinner."

Later that night, the doorbell rang and it was the gardener.

The homeowner asked him, "What's the matter, did you forget something?"

"Nope." replied the gardener, "I'm just here to take your missus out to dinner like you asked."

---

My friend had been asked by his wife to buy some organic vegetables.

When he got to the market garden center he asked the assistant, "These vegetables are for my wife. Have they been sprayed with any poisonous chemicals?"

The assistant answered, "No, you will have to do that yourself."

---

One spring morning, my husband and I were in the garden looking at the flowers we had just planted.

As luck would have it, a bird flew over us leaving his calling card on my clean white shirt.

My husband replied without missing a beat, "You know, Sweetheart, they sing for most folks."

---

Paddy was walking along the street with his friend, Murphy, when a truck drove by fully loaded up with rolls of turf.

Paddy said, "When I win de lottery, I'm gonna do that."

"What exactly is that, Paddy?" responds his friend.

"Send me lawn away to be cut." replied Paddy.

---

Mick decides that he wants to start farming chickens so he buys 100 chicks from a local farmer.

Two weeks later, Mick goes back and buys 50 more.

The following week he goes back to the chicken farmer again and buys another 50 chicks, at which point the chicken farmer says to him, "Your chicken farm must be coming along well now."

Mick looks disheartened and replies, "Unfortunately not. I am just not sure what I'm doing wrong. Maybe I'm planting them too deep, or maybe upside down, or maybe I have just planted them too close together."

---

Patient: Doctor, there's a tulip growing from my ear.

Doctor: That's the strangest thing I have ever heard.

Patient: Yes indeed it is, I planted radishes.

---

A team of gardeners were working outside my house.

I had just finished washing the floor when one of the gardeners asked to use the toilet.

I looked down at his muddy boots and my newly polished floor and I said, "Hang on a second. I'll just put down some newspaper."

"That's all right, madam" he replied. "I'm house trained."

---

Man: 'I'd like a bunch of flowers, please.'

Florist: 'Certainly, sir. What type of flowers would you like?'

Man: 'Umm, I'm not sure.'

Florist: 'Let me help you, sir - what exactly have you done?'

---

A gardener had a roofer called Gary working on his house repairing some tiles.

Gary was up on the roof and accidentally cuts off his ear, and he yelled down to the gardener, "Hey - look out for my ear I just cut off."

The gardener looked around and called up to Gary, "Is this your ear?"

Gary looked down and says, "Nope.  Mine had a pencil behind it!"

---

Paddy sends his Mum a letter.

It reads as follows, "Just letting you I'm in hospital. I accidentally poisoned myself. I ate what I thought was an onion, but it turned out to be a daffodil bulb.  Should be out by spring."

---

A gardener is driving around trying to find an empty space at the gardening store.

"Lord," he prayed. "I really can't stand this much longer. If you open a space up for me, I swear I'll give up the booze and go to church every Sunday."

All of a sudden, a ray of light from the sun beams down onto an empty bay.

Quick as a flash, the gardener says, "Not to worry, Lord, I have found a space."

---

A man visits his doctor's surgery with a parsnip in one ear, a carrot in the other and his nostrils blocked with broad beans.

The doctor tells him, "You need to eat more sensibly."

---

Son: "Dad, do you like baked apples?"

Father: "Yes I do, why do you ask?"

Son: "The orchard's on fire."

---

A dog walks into a pub, and says to the barman, "Can I have a pint of lager and a packet of salted peanuts please."

The barman, who has never heard a talking dog before, says, "That's incredible; you should think about joining the circus.'"

The dog replies, "Why? Do they need gardeners?"

---

The manager of the garden center overhears one of his nurserymen talking to a customer.

'No, we haven't had any of that in ages,' says the nurseryman. 'And I don't know when we'll be getting any more.'

The customer leaves and the manager walks over to give him a telling off.

'Never tell a customer we can't get them something,' he says. 'Whatever they want we can always get it on order and deliver it. Do you understand?'

The nurseryman replies 'OK Boss.'

'So, what did he want?' asks the manager.

'Rain,' replies the nurseryman.

A gardener goes to the doctor complaining about his hearing.

The doctor says, "Can you describe the symptoms to me?"

The gardener replies, "Yes. Homer is a big fat yellow man and his wife Marge is skinny with big blue hair."

---

A gardener meets up with his blonde girlfriend as she's picking up her car from the mechanic.

"Everything ok with your car now?" he asks.

"Yes, thank goodness," the dipsy blonde replies.

He says, "Weren't you worried the mechanic might try to rip you off?"

She replies, "Yes, but he didn't. I was so pleased when he told me that all I needed was blinker fluid!"

---

A new business was opening and one of his friends decided to send him flowers to mark the occasion.

The flowers arrived at the new business and the owner read the card: "Rest in Peace."

The owner was very annoyed, and called the florists to complain.

"Sir, I am very sorry for the mistake, and I am very sorry you feel insulted," said the florist

She continued, "However, at a funeral that is taking place today, there will be a flower arrangement with a card saying, "Congratulations on your new location."

---

A baby hedgehog was lost in the garden. He strolled around until he bumped into a cactus and full of hope he said, "Mum, is that you?"

---

The school cook prided herself on her nutritious meals that she provided which were loaded with vegetables and fruits.

When the power supply failed one day, the cook couldn't serve a hot meal in the cafeteria, so she made up piles of cheese-and-jelly sandwiches.

As one schoolboy filled his plate, he said to his friend, "At last - a home-cooked meal."

---

A gardener calls up her local paper and asks, "How much would it be to put an ad in your paper?"

"It is four dollars an inch," a woman replies. "Why? What are you selling?"

"A four foot step ladder," said the gardener before setting the phone down.

---

A young female gardener is sitting at the bar one night waiting for her friends, when a large sweaty construction worker sits down next to her.

They start talking and after a while they started talking about the worries of nuclear war.

The gardener asks the construction worker, "If you were to hear the sirens go off, know the missiles are on their way, and know you've only got a few minutes left to live, what would you do?"

The construction worker replies, "I will try and make it with anything that moves."

The construction worker then asks the gardener what she would do to which she replies, "I will try and keep perfectly still."

_____

A gardener tries to enter a bar wearing a shirt open at the collar, and is turned away for not having a necktie.

Being a keen gardener had taught him how to be resourceful so goes to his car and makes a tie out of his battery jump leads.

He goes back to the bar and the doorman eyes him up and down and says, "Yes, you can come in now - just don't start anything."

---

A gardener took his cross-eyed Labrador to the vet.

The vet picked the dog up to examine it and said, "Sorry, I'm going to have to put him down."

The gardener cried out, "It's not that bad is it?"

The vet replied, "No, he's just very heavy."

---

## Chapter 5: Longer Gardener Jokes

Henry took over a very old abandoned allotment. The flower beds were completely overgrown with weeds, the shed was in terrible state, and there wasn't much left of the greenhouse apart from the metal frame.

On his first day of work, the local vicar passed by and he said to Henry, "May you and God work hard together to make this the allotment of your dreams."

A few months later, the vicar passed by again and he saw that allotment had been transformed. The shed had been re-built, there were many vegetables were growing in neat rows and the greenhouse had been recently re-glazed and it was full of large plump, ripe marrows.

"That is fabulous," exclaimed the vicar. "Can you see what God and you have achieved together?"

"Yes, I can, Reverend," replied Henry, "but let's not forget the state of the place when God was working on it on his own."

One day a wealthy man was driving along he came across a man at the roadside eating grass.

Disturbed, he stopped and went to investigate.

He asked the man, 'Why are you eating grass?'

'We don't have any money for food,' the man replied. 'So we have to eat grass.'

'In which case you must come with me to my house and I will feed you,' the wealthy man said.

The hungry man said, 'But, sir, I have a wife and two children with me. They are over there, under that tree.'

'They can come too,' the wealthy man replied.

The hungry man called his family over and they all managed to squeeze into the car.

The poor man said to the wealthy man, 'Sir, you are very kind. Thank you so much for taking all of us with you.'

The wealthy gent replied, 'It is my pleasure. You'll really love my place. The grass is almost a foot high.'

A man wants to get his garden fence repaired and following a friend's recommendation he uses a Buddhist monk to do the job.

"It surprised me to see a monk repairing fences," noted the homeowner. "Why do you do it?"

The monk replied, "Religious reasons."

The man then says, "I don't know much about Buddhism. Why do you need to repair fences?"

"Because," the monk replied, "you would be surprised at the amount of karma you get for reposting."

A gardener, a lawyer, a beautiful lady, and an old woman were on a train, sitting 2x2 facing each other.

The train went into a tunnel and when the carriage went completely dark, a loud "thwack" was heard.

When the train came out of the tunnel back into the light the lawyer had a red hand print on his face. He had been slapped on the face.

The old lady thought, "That lawyer must have groped the young lady in the dark and she slapped him."

The hottie thought, "That lawyer must have tried to grope me, got the old lady by mistake, and she slapped him."

The lawyer thought, "That gardener must have groped the hottie, she thought it was me, and slapped me."

The gardener sat there thinking, "I can't wait for another tunnel so I can slap that lawyer again!"

A group of gardeners, all aged 40, discussed where they should meet for a reunion lunch. They agreed they would meet at a place called The Dog House because the barmaids had big breasts and wore short-skirts.

Ten years later, at age 50, the gardeners once again discussed where they should meet for lunch.

It was agreed that they would meet at The Dog House because the food and service was good and there was an excellent beer selection.

Ten years later, at age 60, the friends again discussed where they should meet for lunch.

It was agreed that they would meet at The Dog House because there were plenty of parking spaces, they could dine in peace and quiet, and it was good value for money.

Ten years later, at age 70, the friends discussed where they should meet for lunch.

It was agreed that they would meet at The Dog House because the restaurant was wheelchair accessible and had a toilet for the disabled.

Ten years later, at age 80, the gardeners, now all retired, discussed where they should meet for lunch.

Finally it was agreed that they would meet at The Dog House because they had never been there before.

A pretty woman loved to work in her organic vegetable garden, but no matter what she did, she simply couldn't get her organic tomatoes to ripen at all.

Admiring her neighbor's garden, which had many shiny bright red tomatoes; she asked him what his secret was.

"It's really quite straightforward," the old man explained. "Every morning and every evening, I expose myself in front of the tomatoes and they turn red with embarrassment."

Desperate for the perfect organic garden, she decided to follow his advice and she then proceeded to expose herself to her plants twice a day.

A few weeks passed and her neighbor popped by to check on the progress of her garden.

"So," he asked, "Have you had any luck with your tomatoes?"

"No," she replied breathlessly, "but you should see the size of my cucumbers."

Ron is talking to two of his friends, Jim and Shamus.

Jim says, "I think my wife is having an affair with a gardener. The other day I came home and found a trowel under our bed and it wasn't mine."

Shamus then confides, "Wow, me too! I think my wife is having an affair with an electrician. The other day I found wire cutters under the bed and they weren't mine."

Ron thinks for a minute and then says, "You know what, I think my wife is having an affair with a horse."

Both Jim and Shamus look at him in complete disbelief.

Ron sees them looking at him and says, "No, I mean it. The other day I came home early and found a jockey under our bed."

A passer-by came across an old man who was crying his eyes out, so he asked him what the problem is.

"Well," said the old chap. "For many years, I was a landscape gardener, and I managed to sell my business a few years ago for quite a large sum of money."

The passer-by said, "That's great. So why are you crying?"

The old man moaned, "I now own a very large house."

The passer-by said, "Yes, so why are you crying?"

The old chap sobbed and said, "I own a lovely car."

The passer-by said, "So tell me why are you crying?"

The old man weeped, "A few months ago I married a young glamour model."

The passer-by demanded, "So what exactly is the problem?"

The old chap sniffled, "I just can't remember where I live.

Carlo the property developer and his gardener buddy Doug, went bar-hopping most weekends together, and most weeks Carlo would go home with a hot woman while Doug went home alone.

One week Doug asked Carlo what his secret was to picking up women.

"It's easy," said Carlo "When a woman asks you what you do for a living, don't tell her you're a gardener. Tell her you're a lawyer instead."

Later Doug is chatting with a fit older woman when she leans in and asks him what he does for a living.

"I'm a lawyer," says Doug.

The woman smiles and asks, "Want to go back to my place? It's just around the corner."

So they go to her place, have some fun and an hour or so later, Doug is back in the pub telling Carlo about his success.

"I've only been a lawyer for an hour," Doug snickered, "And I've already screwed someone!"

A male gardener was talking to two of his friends about their teenage daughters.

The first friend says, "I was cleaning my daughter's room the other day and I found a pack of cigarettes. I didn't even know she smoked."

The second friend says, "That's nothing. I was cleaning my daughter's room the other day and I found a half full bottle of Vodka. I didn't even know she drank."

The gardener says, "That's nothing. I was cleaning my daughter's room the other day and I found a pack of condoms. I didn't even know she had a penis."

An 85 year old gardener was walking through the local park one day when he came across a frog.

He reached down, picked the frog up, and started to put it in his pocket.

As he did so, the frog said, "Kiss me on the lips and I will turn into a beautiful woman and give you the time of your life."

The old gardener carried on putting the frog in his pocket.

The frog said, "Didn't you hear what I said?"

The gardener looked back at the frog and said, "Yes, but at my age I think I'd rather have a talking frog."

## Chapter 6: Gardener Pick-Up Lines

Warning - some of these are quite risqué!

---

You smell like a freshly cut lawn.

---

My roses aren't the only things with long stems.

---

Can I interest you in some of my compost?

---

Can I rake your front yard?

---

Can I trim your bush?

---

Want to talk dirty with me?

---

Girl, you smell like lavender.

---

How about we plant seeds together?

---

How about you and me turnip in your bed?

---

Want to see how big my squash grows?

---

Don't worry; I'm 100% organic and locally grown.

---

How juicy are your pummelos?

---

How long has it been since you mowed your lawn?

---

## Chapter 7: Bumper Stickers for Gardeners

Sometimes I wet my plants.

---

I fought the lawn and the lawn won.

---

I dig worms.

---

There are two kinds of people in the world. Gardeners and those who wish they were.

---

Gardening helps you hide bodies.

---

My best friend is a hoe.

---

## Chapter 8: Summary

Hey, that's pretty well it for this book. I hope you've enjoyed this collection of gardeners jokes. As you know, some were corny, and some you may have heard before; but I hope they brought a smile to your face.

I've written a few other joke books for other professions. Here are just a few sample jokes; these are from my electricians joke book:-

---

Q: What is the definition of a shock absorber?

A: A careless electrician.

---

Q: What kind of van does an electrician drive?

A: A Volts-wagon.

---

Q: What do you call a Russian electrician?

A: Switchitonanov.

---

## About The Author

Chester Croker has written many joke books, and the inspiration for this one came from his mother who just loves her plants, and spends more time in the garden than she does indoors.

Chester has twice been voted Comedy Writer of the Year by the International Jokers Guild.

If you see anything wrong, or you have a gag you would like to see included in the next version of this book, please visit the glowwormpress.com website.

If you did enjoy the book, kindly leave a review on Amazon so that other gardeners can have a good laugh too.

Thanks in advance.

Printed in Great Britain
by Amazon

43815666R00037